Egg Island Almanac

For Mike,
Best of Luck!

POEMS BY

BRENDAN GALVIN

Brendan

Crab Orchard Review &
Southern Illinois University Press
Carbondale

Southern Illinois University Press
www.siupress.com

20   19   18   17   4   3   2   1

The Crab Orchard Series in Poetry is a joint publishing venture
of Southern Illinois University Press and *Crab Orchard Review*.
This series has been made possible by the generous support of
the Office of the President of Southern Illinois University and the
Office of the Vice Chancellor for Academic Affairs and Provost at
Southern Illinois University Carbondale.

Editor of the Crab Orchard Series in Poetry: Jon Tribble
Judge for the 2016 Open Competition Award: Maura Stanton

Cover illustration: photo taken by author (cropped)

Library of Congress Cataloging-in-Publication Data
Names: Galvin, Brendan, author.
Title: Egg island almanac / poems by Brendan Galvin.
Description: Carbondale : Crab Orchard Review & Southern
Illinois University Press, 2017. | Series: Crab Orchard Series
in Poetry
Identifiers: LCCN 2017001043 | ISBN 9780809336074
(paperback) | ISBN 9780809336081 (e-book)
Subjects: | BISAC: POETRY / General.
Classification: LCC PS3557.A44 A6 2017 | DDC 811/.54—dc23
LC record available at https://lccn.loc.gov/2017001043

For Ellen Baer Galvin (1935–2014),
in loving memory.

"We had so much fun together."

CONTENTS

Egg Island
Almanac

ORDNANCE

Ever see one of these before?
McDaid tossed me a hard plug,
weightier than the ignorance

I'd attached like a water balloon
to the phrase "rubber bullet."

It's January now, but winter and summer
I keep coming across these balloons

flashing colors like visual noise
in the marshes, and in pine groves
that trap their sheen.

Bobbing and nodding, candy-apple red,
this one is metallic, tangled and raising
its black-and-white eyeballs to high heaven

from thickets surrounding the kettle pond.
It couldn't shatter a kneecap or femur
like the ordnance on McDaid's kitchen table.

Set free to advertise some birthday boy
important enough to inflict his name

and shiny future on a south-facing
arrangement of water and trees,
this time of year this balloon

may never get to strangle a turtle,
let alone get sucked down
the blowhole of a dolphin.

DUETS

During the blizzard, before the wren came,
I was not thinking about islands with bananaquits
and frigate birds and an occasional taste
of the local rum. Of all those eighty million
Americans under that red zone on
the weather channel, I thought only
of you on Stage Harbor, My Love.

Things began appearing in twos.
Foxes first, after the seeds and suet crumbs
knocked from the feeders by wind,
one light-footing it over the dunes of snow,
a parent perhaps, lush in its color and coat,
and the second maybe a shaggy youngster.

Rumpled twins next, a duet of bluebirds
on the deck rail, the wind still thumping, then
a downy woodpecker on one side
of the hanging suet cake and on the other
the wren, a Carolina by its white supercilium.

Anything else with wings kept the house
between it and that banging wind, but the wren
puffed up on a branch like a tennis ball
that spent last week in a retriever's mouth.
Then to the suet for more. The wren
like a high-rise window cleaner swinging,
the walkway dangling loose.

Finally the woodpecker escaped through a scrim
of ocean-effect snow. The bluebirds and foxes

already vanished, I promised I would be here
for you alone, Love, persistent as the wren,
who kept coming back, wind be damned, this storm's
emblem for heart, chipping that suet cake to a slice
thin as morning toast while the night kept coming.

SEEING STARS

J'ai appris que les morts ne quittent jamais les vivant.
—Philippe Claudel

Was I twelve when that girl's hand
first came shyly over my shoulder
from the row behind, the B-flick
love story conning us both? Above us
the gum-wrapper foils were shooting
across the Rialto's projector beam
like meteorites to wish a future on.
Whatever her name was, we were
too young for her to be one of the women
I vowed to change every cell of my
nature for, though later there were
a few collisions of equal and opposite
outlooks, two crimped faces spurting
self-regard like oil, two voices
leaking steam under a moon we created
so we could howl it down. I needed you
to pry the rocks from my hands. Thank you
for never looking at me these forty-eight years
as though I were some fish who just
walked into our house on my new feet.
Though I know where reason says
you should be, on the first night
of the blizzard I climbed into
your hospital bed in the living room
for only the hint of you that might
yet be there. And again the second night,
but this evening as the snow moves off
you are here with me again. You look in

at me for this quarter hour of sunset,
companionable star, and I at you,
Dear Love, knowing where you are
as you travel the sky-space
between two pine crowns.

FIRST IMPRESSIONS

If these were sand dunes I could tell you
which prints were a coyote's or fox's
or dog's, but they're dunes in a fresh-fallen
snowscape dashed by anything fleeing the cold.
Take these imprints with nothing between
them but white space. No feet, as though
someone kept dropping and retrieving
a computer mouse and cord. A leaper,
for sure, but since they are hibernators
it wasn't a jumping mouse. Maybe
a white-footed. Or a house mouse,
that despised one who allegedly performs
a birdlike overture while courting,
a song you can hear if you're real close,
they claim, and why not? It's as possible
as that time years ago when I collared my dog
as he stood over a screaming cottontail.
Both could be as true as this weather that's
tweaking the house like a nutcracker for a way in.

LIMBO

Two in the troughs the wind made
in snow drifting across the deck,
taking their chances since yesterday
for sunflower seeds the cardinals
and chickadees knock from the feeder,

two bobwhite quail who bail out
but fly back again because there are
feet of snow over my brush piles
where they might have a chance—

her dead-grass yellowish throat
and eyestreak, their colors of winter oak leaf
and snow-striped branches—

against the red-tailed hawks and that yearling
coyote I saw floating up the fireroad,
so quick it barely touched down
long enough to leave snowprints.

Given what comes from the air
without warning, and out of the marshes,
I know that longevity means nothing
for them, but where are they? All day the souls
of children in Limbo have troubled me,

that savage human neverland
that's too much theology for a handful
of feathers defending a heartbeat
while this white absence rumbles through.

TO A FRUIT FLY IN WINTER

A splash of Oban on the rocks had me
traveling in mind to its namesake ferry port,
the way out to Mull and Barra—Oban,

with McCaig's unfinished Colosseum
on the hill above the harbor, a scheme to bring
honest labor to nineteenth-century crofters.

Then you appeared on the edge of my
single-malted breath, *Drosophila
melanogaster*, black-bellied dew lover.

I had thought to rid the house of your kind
by leaving the compost bucket open
outside for a minute to the January stars,

watching the lot of you ascend to vanishing
a foot above the rim, poor astronauts.

Though I cannot order you to visit the neighbors
the way my old-country grandmother
commanded the radio, sick of its blather,

I fixed a glass of Fly Wine, red plonk
doctored with a drop of detergent
to break the surface tension so you'd drown,

even shut the oven door and hit the bake buttons
after you'd spent the night inside
carousing on banana peels,

but here you are, apparently immortal,
drawn to my Oban's West Highland
bouquet, a dew lover indeed.

A JANUARY HERON

If you were really Camerarius's
emblem of the wise man who takes steps
against misfortune, you wouldn't
be here today. You're not
the medieval stand-in for
the oversexed, either, unless
this river ice colored like the sky
promotes abstinence.

Whisky weather, and you're grounded
over there like the negative
of a marsh-side cedar, puffed
feathers maximizing insulation.
Close enough, I think I might hear
this wind piping down
your hollow bones.

For your allegiance to this place
where the osprey's only a rumor,
in my *Speculum Mundi*
or *Wild Guess at the World*
you have the power of remembering
beyond geese who splayfoot it down
only when the water's open,
and the second sight to project
yourself lifting sideways out of
this marsh, displaying
a Jurassic shape to summer.

POST OFFICE PARKING LOT, FEBRUARY

Age doesn't come to call,
but knocks us into side-angle-side
whiteheads and blue hairs with canes.
As the wind adds an extra stagger
to my step, I think of you, Turkana Boy,
rescued two million years too late
from the sediments around a Kenyan lake
and given its name, your real name
among the savanna dwellers
probably unable to be spoken, maybe
some ornate motion of a hand in the air.

You seemed to spring upright and modern
in your body, nothing remotely as human
before you, proof of Huxley's view
that Nature makes jumps. Not one of us
in this parking lot earned our gait
dodging the big cats of the grasslands
or snatching a child from one, more likely
from living on the clock under gravity.
Falling out of bilateral symmetry,
I keep you in mind as sand falls
through my hourglass and I move like
I just fell out of a tree,
trying my luck on the ground.

CABIN FEVER

1.

That candidate whose face on TV
seemed a mattress abandoned
to his spirit's vacant lot
drove me out to the woodpile.

Breaking into rounds of cold oak,
trying not to think of meretricious
skulls, I gave up and set the axe aside,
and began listening to the grove

creaking here and there, the slight
groans and sighs of pitch pines and oaks,
the breeze weaving higher branches
together, locusts playing off one another,

a reasonable music, neither
electronic nor human, until a redbelly
began heckling from a pine crown,
a reminder to gather my splits

and build a fire in the stove before
the first flakes, to knot up "Metro"
and "Sunday Styles" before snow
oversimplified the paths and woodshed,

to attend the flames as though
back in a time when humanity
had little as companionable.

2.

The blizzard inside the hurricane,
or is it the hurricane inside the blizzard?
In all this banging and flapping
a god within another god has ordered

the spruces to bow down and peppered
these windows with salt spray. Can there be
an "I" in this storm surge rolling the coast
over until stumps of that ancient cedar swamp

appear briefly again, proof that the sea
when it's ready will take us back, as the air
and its waters took the cedar fence posts back.
What of the juncos and nuthatches out there

exploring interstices of ice, the sparrows
and chickadees in their workaday coveralls?
The light dives for zero, and the clock
drips each second like a plumber's nightmare.

Time to consider how far those birds have flown
from *T. rex*. In the woodstove window a face
keeps appearing, almost familiar. We too
are made of carbon and flames.

It's as strange as someone gluing a human head
onto the middle ape in a timeline picture
demonstrating the stages from beast to hominid,

the way this peacock struts among the ranks
of eleven wild turkeys, the local flock,
spreading his fan like a stained-glass window
you'd think his envious drab cousins
would try to fly right through.

He likes his lovin' on the exotic side,
declares a man we call the Passionate Plumber,
and Mrs. Baker claims he attacked the colors
of her dress, says he's the Judas you'll find in any dozen,
and won't scatter split corn for him

as Mrs. Caruso does, so he comes running
to her porch, mornings when the troop's
in her neighborhood, and will wait for her there.

Some are remembering that Mexican parrot,
its lime-green vivid as its screech all one fall
against our pines, and that pit bull who wintered over
in the National Seashore.
                         One even claims
to have seen something prehistoric on the beach,
which is perhaps to say
it's your own fault if your day is dull.

Peafowl strays show up from India, the books report,
but I'm betting on some fop's summer garden,
McMansion and bird abandoned
for Greenwich or Darien.

February now, and things no one can wait for or predict
climb out of the ordinary
nut-rich hollows, cross the roads, fly in a low line
over marsh grass, and we stop
breathless and look, lavishly bushwhacked.

Along the route fall took
four months ago,
something is loping
cross-field toward you,
getting barked off farms.
The first plover of the year
knows it and takes off
piping like a cork
worked in a bottleneck,
and now you will have to
stand your ground alone
while something forces
thickets, splashing among
dead leaves, and half white,
half mud, a heap of old snow,
the runt of the litter
looks back once, heading north.

There is no radical shift of light
or redwings calling areas of marsh
their territories yet, nor plovers
probing for copepods. Only a yellow
front-end loader laying out a new berm
on the beach, from tubes too heavy
to be called hoses, its audience one man
and his protesting dog. No frosted
wedding cake on tour, no Cap'n
Beauregard hailing us from
the Texas deck, no Texas deck,
just an unshaven crew launching zodiacs
from the county dredge, its twin stacks
staining itself and the air with smoke,
as battered an emblem of hope as any other.
So spring comes to Egg Island, squealing
and unwilling. Sulfur and diesel,
flywheel, gear and grind until one morning
the equinox dawns and silences
the whole shebang.

A SEA PIECE

That snowy owl up on the moors,
using an electrical meter box
for her rodent stand—what sense
does she make of the disc
that's turning beneath her feet,
the annular way of things?

Even this dowel stamped with
numbers must mean something
somewhere, but tumbled onto
the winter beach it's a mere
synecdoche for a list or logbook,
like all those initialed and coded
parts bumbling around out there
with no one to decipher them.

Marconi late in life believed
that every attempt at speech
was up there yet in sound waves
going around the earth, waiting
to be tapped into by the future's
headphones, but never concluded
that such a babel of tongues mostly
lost would be heard as gibberish.

ASTONISHMENT

When it arrives, it's more likely
to seem a sparrow bedraggled by
three days of rain than some
day-glo lightning bolt, a wild
underhang of feathers
below its tricolor brown, black
and white. Until you notice
it's way too hefty, the beak is
pink and wrong, and that's not
the sparrow's grab-and-go at
the feeder: it is hanging around
as if lost, a blow-in on a northeast
storm who has followed the locals
to a seed source, its white eyestripe
and lunula at first perhaps
a Sam Peabody bird's, only then
the astonishment that it may be
from Thule or Flatey. Though it
matches up with photos
of stragglers to the Aleutians
and Orkneys, there's been
no sighting of its kind here ever.
Ordinary where it lives, for an hour
it's a godsend from the marvelous,
not for anyone caught in
a type A life list competition.

THE JACKRABBIT'S EARS

*It is a damn poor mind indeed which can't think of at least
two ways to spell any word.*

—Andrew Jackson

*The years ar [sic] placed at the upper part of the head and
very near to each other.*

—Meriwether Lewis

And grow nearer as we grow older, with memory
up there entangling events and revising faces,
reaching into the story that will be our lives,
though the years are very flexible
and have been known to sponsor surprises,
a hurricane in December, blizzards in May,
and weathers that trip outlandish blossomings.

The front outer fold of the year is a reddish brown,
except one inch at the tip of the year that is black,
though I can remember whole blue years
that seemed like exhaustive studies
in roadside gravel, and that black inch
should be fair warning the next twelve months
won't be a romp through the Kingdom of the Sun.

When the years are thrown back they don't break down
and recycle like compost, returning themselves
to us a day at a time, but more like boomerangs
they startle with their sudden reprises of people,
scenes, ancient slights either magnified
or better understood, and the motives of others
coming clearer with time.

Meriwether Lewis, you were the first
to describe the Hare of the Prairie or jackrabbit
fleet enough to be Time's logo. Spelling be damned,
you breathed air clearer than anyone will again,
saw buffalo herds without apparent end,
and worked with Thomas Jefferson,

yet given to melancholy, you died young
on the Natchez Trace, probably by
your own hand, as though you saw
how the years were like that yellow bear
of Montana, gutshot and lungshot, who stayed
in the chase and would not fail.

LEFTY'S GAME

Maybe you wouldn't call it
a ball game, but there's a red ball
and he gets all four feet
four feet or more off the ground
when it's necessary to field it,
and one time in twenty
will deliver it back to my hand.

Sometimes he just drops it
and loops through the pine grove,
lopes the route he's worn
among berry bushes and scrub,
dead-aimed at the ball,

and other times charges me
showing no ball, but serious teeth,
like he's going to eat me up,
a move converted from
canine memory into play.

As he passes close I slap his back
to reward this work he's created
for himself, as other border collies
have invented their own games,
no rules we understand,

no sense of innocence or wrong
for us to work around, just a few
personal habits to be acknowledged,
and the look in his eyes when
he catches me singing "Shenandoah."

THE FISH CROWS

As the alewives arrive,
the forsythia lights itself,
and soon shadbush will whiten
by the rivers where shad appear.

But what's the signal for fish crows?
Me, apparently, splitting my last
layer of firewood as a weak
note, a tinny *yawk*

sounds above me, then its echo,
kazoo-like, then all the guests
leaving a New Year's party,
blowing their toy horns
though it's nearly April.

Fish crows: usually one or two
will be traveling with their larger cousins,
who keep above it all, out of range,
or loiter in the breakdown lane.

But here for the first time in my
three quarters of a century
is a whole flock of fish crows
celebrating a new beginning.

Hard to imagine them unwrapping
grief like a gift on a morning like this,
corporeal subdividers like their
relatives, while the lilacs

prepare to announce that bluebacks
are beginning to thread their way
up the herring runs.

TOTEMS

I live between the heron and the wren.
——Theodore Roethke

Maybe I should downsize and opt for the wren
at my age, though the heron enlisted me
on a May afternoon in 1965. North Pamet Road,
delivering shrubbery for a landscaper,

a great blue in that kettle pond
by the overgrown cranberry bog, tallest
and stillest, the genius of the place.
That day I knew distractions would not
be fatal to my hopes here.

The wren is disarming though, lifting
its throat and letting go at the sky
so you have to clutch in surprise
whatever you're holding. I love how
at nesting time its warning buzz can make
strangers look around for the rattlesnake.

Would it be presumption or even desertion
to shift my needs onto it? It must weigh
only about as much as the heron's
kneecap, and the great blue is perfect for
the flat, long trip across distance,
the overview, its *cronk* matter-of-fact.

If I go quietly in winter the heron
may hold its ground twenty feet away.
Never have I had a bad day with one sailing
on the margins——it can mean good mail
at the P.O. that afternoon, for instance.

Ah, but the wren goes here and there,
twitching at details among the haiku tidbits,
and it's only the owl Mutterkin who demands
from the grove that I choose which of the two.

At roadside this morning the discarded
paper latte cups outnumbered
the empty nips of Jim Beam. Summer
was well on its way, and shortly
a whirring person, mantis-thin,
appeared on a bicycle scrolled with
a flow of vowels approximating
Aeolia, a vehicle slim as a stringed
instrument designed and tuned by
a maestro of silver microtools,
its rider wrapped up tight
as if in the flags of several principalities.
Under the myrmidon helmet
he took on a visage as he passed
without a nod and disappeared
up the road, no doubt to dismount
and face off against a monstrous affliction
somewhere, while I stood among
the new yellowthroats and fiddleheads,
hearing the first black-billed
cuckoo of the year and wondering
whether a walk
is always only a walk.

This wild tom picking his way
along the roadside looks as
absurd and un-American
as the grand recessional
of a royal wedding, and seems
unaware that his black cloak,
set against that forsythia's
pyrotechnics, makes a target.

What were you thinking, Ben,
when you nominated the wild turkey
for our national bird? That any
purblind musketeer could
bring down that family-size
hump of light and dark meat?

He's out here under the aegis of Fish
and Game, but looks as unaffiliated
as Baba Yaga, her hut aloft
on bony legs, herself her home,
until he lifts that blue
question mark of neck and head,
and in self-doubt appears composed
of parts a Yankee farmer grafted
cleverly enough to charge admission.

Ego-involved yourself, first foxy
grandfather of the republic,
did you foresee how fledged with
self-regard we'd become, our country
stepping out like him,
as confident as any true believer
bearing that pageantry onto Route 6?

The jays seemed to work from nine to five
and break for an hour around noon,
both of them bringing snippets
of last year's bean runners, dried catbriar,
fragments of rootlet and bine,
which she worried into shape as though
weaving a beard for that pine trunk
twenty feet from this window. When
the nestlings broke into this world,
skinheads, pink omnivorous yawps,
their father stood guard. Not fondly,
I'd surmise from his barbed head, but not
shrieking either, on a branch he'd
otherwise issue threats from. The way
he sat in on the nest for her looked like
rudimentary parenthood—as if they could
turn and live the way we do. He held her
in his regard so you'd think he saw
bark scale and sky and moss tuning
themselves to her jay blues. Berserkers,
she wasn't long kept from spearing
a foreign egg clutch, and he'd rip away
at some little flower of carnage pinned
with his feet. One day the empty nest
looked not quite like absolute zero, but ratty
and somehow Whitmanian, as though
the good gray poet himself had invented
this whole arrangement, then hung
his beard in the tree and gone home.

THE JUNE LIGHT IN LOCUST GROVES

If you will believe that these robins and catbirds
drunkenly wobbling from the feast of
the trees' solstitial flowering
are blinking as though to dispel much more
than those little weddings before their eyes,

I will believe you have seen a woman
fixing blossoms in her hair, and grinding corn,
and a man chipping a tool from a likely stone.

When you said you had dreamed one night
that the Algonquians were readying for winter
in this south-facing hollow again,

where each fall we chunk out
the dead locust trunks that will glow
like ingots in our stove, trying to bake
lifetimes of Atlantic weather
from our bones, I knew

it wasn't only the grass fed by nitrogen-fixing
bacteria in the nodes of locust roots
that creates this light on June evenings.

There must be a midden of oystershell
and fishbones under this grove
where you saw those first people

moving among houses of woven mat
above the turtle pond, and crouched at a fire pit
lined with stones those ancient cook-fires
turned orange and pink, and speaking
a tongue no one living
has heard in his waking life.

REBUILDING A WOODPILE AT THE SUMMER SOLSTICE

in memory of George Garrett

It must be a strain of residual Yankee in me, that advises
it's best to prepare for whatever eventualities
we can, though I won't climb to the flue to plunge
and retrieve a wire brush until cold has caught the bees.

Things turned elegiac when I began to play
a memory game with the garden,
stacking one split of oak for the squash plants
laying their trip wires a month from here,

then an elbow of applewood for bean blossoms like
the beesting lips on old movie vamps,
and one log for that insect I spot two or three times
a summer, that looks like a spark plug

with wires twisted on for legs and antennae,
its buzz and crackle suggesting technology.
So it went, top to bottom, no sign of rodent nests
or a coachwhip snake hauling its braid out of sight.

Prying the bottom layer, there was bleached grass,
and roly-poly bugs, mushroom territory come September.
I should have done this on a day when frost was curing
the final pole beans to strips of leather.

Lord, if it's possible for those seeming originals
to rise out of punkwood and sawdust for a few days,
I mean the mushroom like an orange on a stick
and the one like a brass-studded leather biker's cap,

29

maybe it's possible that after my longest flight,
in need of fortification, I'll walk into a paneled lounge
as I did once at Logan Airport and your servant
George will turn from the bar again
with the sun in his smile and a new story.

CAPERCAILLIE

We're going to walk in and come around
behind them this morning, and drive them before us
out toward the car park, he says,
slate-blue birds the size of American turkeys,
fast on the ground, with noisy flapping takeoffs.
He's never not seen them here
in this nook of the Grampians, so we step off
smartly behind his shouldered scope and tripod.

They'll tilt between these
thick pines, spectacular,
their cries like someone retching,
then a pulled-cork pop ending
in a rhythmic wheezing gargle.
Sway-bellied,
a half mile in he's huffing himself
lobster-faced under his deerstalker cap,
a home guard in some
J. Arthur Rank farce, defending his village
against the Axis. Everybody happy?
Everybody happy? We believe only in
the pursuit of happiness, Mrs. Darby mumbles
at him, and not in the capercaillie,
though she's bird-ready
from her tweed cap to her suction-cup soles.

Now he's after us to keep quiet,
spread out and skirt the bog
to its end, then we'll turn
and herd them before us.
Red Highland cattle's
the only herd an hour later.
Unfenced, postcard-ready,

but in truth cutely disposed
to use their horns.
Weak eyes in every shaggy head,
I'm praying, and—Christ Jesus!—he's in
the bog to his knees, crashing tussock
to tussock, arm-waving us to spread out
as we make the trees and turn.

Alert for croak, pop, wheeze, gurgle,
we've lost Mrs. Darby somewhere in our rising
and dropping across the knolls another hour,
until the lost graveyard of
cannibalized lorries, fenderless Morrises,
mixed spruce and birch thriving
through yawns of bonnet and door—
and Mrs. Darby waiting to say
there is no such bird as the capercaillie,
"horse of the woods."
It's only the Scots' envy of our turkey,
and the Gaelic name translates
for her to "goosechase," related to
deerstalker's pals over single malts
chewy with Spey water and peat after we've gone.

And to "snipe hunt" for me:
I am a tenderfoot with flashlight
and burlap bag again, crouched in a midnight
thicket of memory, except here comes
a chaffinch, gray-blue helmeted,
commonest of its kind,
to wait at my feet for any crumb,
its salmon-colored breast offering
a change of heart, to follow me anywhere.

JULY HAILSTORM

Because I remembered New Orleans after
a five-day rain, Canal Street and Tchoupitoulas
stocked with wading spoonbills
and ibises out of the bayous, even a few
unidentifiables spinning and jumping in puddles,

I went down to the marsh behind Egg Island
at first light, the clouds such scumbled mixes,
such baroque scrollworks and smears
I couldn't tell you if they were
cirrostratus or nimbocumulus.

I went to the shell flats hoping for more than
just the usual courage of terns
in the face of a buzzard over their
nesting grounds, because after 3 A.M.
a wind had begun trying

as if by osmosis to draw the bedroom curtains
through the screens, then lightning,
thunder, then something on the roof and skylights
like bushels of marbles poured,
cat's-eyes and agates rattling.

I thought of those pellets rising
and falling in the storm, building
layer by layer so at dawn
there were holes in my squash plants.

Back of Egg Island the sand had been pocked
and pummeled to a new softness, and I scared up
a pied blow-in, chocolate and white, who beat it
for the river on wings heavily chevroned—

oystercatcher, rarity enough so I played
a mild game of hockey on the way home,
with my blackthorn stick
helped a puck-size snapping turtle
to the far side of the road it appeared headed for.

STRIVERS' MOON

Insects are laying down their high-tension trills
this dog day evening, under a full moon
riding a cloud stream, coin of that
unattainable realm,
and down here a squash blossom's
trying to reflect it.

The beans are up their poles and above,
aspiring moonward, wavering, trying for
a handhold of air, and the thistles are working
themselves into lavender frazzles
to rise to this stellar occasion.

Year in, year out, they leave their failures
behind them. Even this pine,
which should have broken itself
decades ago from leaning at that angle,
has never entertained surrender.

Meanwhile, in the nether zones,
borers, aphids, suckers, hornworms,
diptera and beetles patrol, trying
to shut any aspirations down.

Go for it anyway, you gumweeds
and sunflowers, you maypops and star
cucumbers. Reach for that cosmic
doubloon. Show those green weenies
and hunchbacks of piety how it's done.

REVENANT

I was thinking about weed-whacking the path
when something large dropped onto
the tip of that dead tree thirty yards from
the window. The usual redtail?

There was no posse of jays or blackbirds. Then
the barbed head that bursts the surface of bays
registered, and the severe billhook,
and only then the osprey's black and white.

It leaned and began tearing whatever was pinned
in its feet, turned it so I could make out
the silver of fish belly. From time to time it
looked directly at me, plucking the flesh,

apparently not threatened by binoculars.
"Fish Hawk," of course,
no other nickname but its function.

Revenant from its chemical oblivion, fish gone,
it cleaned and groomed itself. Was it so apparitional
before DDT? They say a poultryman
might mount a wagon wheel on a pole back then

so the fish hawk could construct its elaborate nest
up there and drive off any chicken hawks,
saving its young and the farmer's,
which it had no taste for.

FORTUNE COOKIE

When I drew out the message it advised,
To truly find yourself you should
play hide-and-seek alone. I remembered
sounds like the first few drops of rain
that morning—a yellowthroat
tapping at the trapezoid windows,
indignant in his domino mask, defending
his nest in the maple against
his own reflection, beating himself up
with his wings. Years since a towhee
used to do that, and at least
this yellow flutterer didn't mark the glass
with the towhee's script, an alphabet
housing an augury passed on
from some wanderers apparently
gone extinct on the underbelly of Asia.

Forty-nine degrees and you were
already here at the garden pool,
a double-handful in your pickerel skin,
as though at that rung of being
there's a universal coverall.

I didn't see you when I raked out
last year's leaves and piled them on
the compost, then I did, there on the rim
as if you knew I was about
an improvement on your behalf.

Now I do. Even when I switch on
the pump you are silent and unmoved,
though there's panic among
the water striders, and even
smaller things are in motion.

Your look is noncommittal,
an elderly pawnbroker's face,
or pond-breaker's when
with a glunk I hear you enter
the water. Gerontion,

that's what I call you, because
at night I have heard you saying over
and over like the best-read
frog ever, *Gerontion, Gerontion.*

AN INCH OF ELECTRIC GREEN

for Ellen

It leapt in through a dashboard louver
onto the passenger seat. Grasshopper,
delicate as a dress accessory you might wear.

Did I own a neon windbreaker that color
sixty years ago, could I have been
that gauche? And if not, where
had I seen that shade of green before?

Through the traffic of four or five towns
and the skirting of three bays and a few coves,
that virid bug kept taking me to memory's
greener venues: the we-can-do-it
of the garden's pumpkin leaves, for instance,

and among the leaps of recollection,
how the North Sea forbids grasshoppers
farther passage than Hoy, tallest of the Orkneys.

And for no other reason I can fathom than
the bug's range of motion, before its italic limbs
finally sprung it out the open window
I recalled that day going past the drive-in theatre

when we saw the man who'd had a stroke like yours,
the one I held up as an example while he pushed
along the sidewalk by the state road, struggling
himself back toward a younger self.

But failed, apparently, since I'd seen him
a few times later in a motorized wheelchair,
a hankie-sized red flag waggling his presence
in the breakdown lane. I kept that to myself,

and it was only yesterday I could tell you
he was on his own two feet again at the drugstore,
gray as we are, but almost dashing with
his cane and belted leather coat.

It will happen on the day I look down
at blue and magenta leaves
which are probably auto air fresheners
thrown onto the roadside, or the day
I take the long slide on a fatal
slice of lime tossed among the kayaks
racked like so many spiritual
ventures. High summer,
Mr. and Mrs. Eugenides in their
red vacation-rental convertible,
the whole town become an ego
theme park, and I'll want to follow
the fox's elegant footprints out across
the sandy apron under the pine duff
and beg admission. But the foxprints
will be gone, and the fox,
knowing enough to hole up
and wait out this all too-human
season, and I'll fill a pocket
with sunflower seeds and take
myself into the beechwoods
that defend a pond of water lilies
lit like white candles and scenting
the heat with licorice. On the path
I'll hold out both palms like
a garden statue, thinking Brother
Chickadee, Sister Chickadee, but
sounding like *pish, pish, pish,*
until one from nowhere clamps
a finger—the Franciscan moment—
taking its time, hunting judiciously
for just the right seed, passing
its grip down to me,
a strength, a way of holding on.

41

VOLUNTEERS

Having attained critical mass
these scalloped pattypans
are waiting for me by the door,
and over there are runners
strung with still other
varieties of squash. Variously
ribbed or warty, flattened
like hubcaps, globed, green-striped
on ivory and vice versa, they have
strayed off on tendrils for
the compass points while I was
visiting down the hemisphere
instead of hoeing and weeding.

If I count them now I will get
a different census entirely
tomorrow. Not one from a seed
tucked into last May's rototilled bed,
their vines have crawled from
the business of forty-eight years'
compost. Survivors of scoop, dump,
toss and drop, they're escaping
themselves by passing themselves on,
free-range theologians with their
faith in the risen dust.

And now our artisanal baker skims
his black beret like a frisbee across
the patisserie, and reverts to English major.
His Inspector Clouseau accent drops away.
Donning his Sox cap, he locks the door,
sees so many spoked wheels turn
in the salty air, then a motor and zodiac,
then a couple of plastic kayaks that look
like genetically wrangled bananas.
As he passes the Custom Design Center
he knows it's over, it's back to the city
where the sofas are never called
ambience furnishings. These landscapers'
trailers are wider than pickup beds
and loaded with jet skis, a Harley,
assorted surfboards, collapsed
beach umbrellas. They move with others
toward the sand dunes and bridge at
fourteen mph, as though in a pageant
of ownership. Where is the creative
director, he wonders, and the prospectus
of restaurant profiles, the rich fabric of nightly
festivals with coveted five-star ratings?
The year-rounders are getting their town
and native language back. Everyone else is
heading away from this place before
it heads out to winter at sea. There will be
no potlatch, no grand giveaway
of their things, and now he remembers
the Joads in that movie, their vehicle
wobbly with lashed-on needs, and thinks
there is more than one kind of poverty.

QUESTIONS OF TRAVEL?

Where are the june bugs that hit
the screens strumming on spring evenings
years ago, and the brown creepers
that went up and down pine trunks
disguised as bark in motion?

Gone, and the whip-poor-wills going,
and the evening grosbeaks that used to
arrive like a flock of windblown
gas station pennants. The cod are
going fast, and the quail,

but when I weed-whack the path to the pond
in June, I still come upon blossoming
foxgloves, still surprised at their bells
shaped like the earpieces of wall phones
seen only in old movies now.

From one spring to the next they are never
where I expect them, as though they have
powers. Science can explain it as the scatter
of a few million seeds from each
short-lived plant, and the requisite acidic soil.

Lady slippers too are based on such needs,
their rare sheep's-head shape good for a month
then gone, only to arrive elsewhere another year
when underwritten by the appropriate fungus.

So much for June, but now it's September,
and this morning I came over the hill to find
a skinny fox staring me down from the road's
yellow line, as though I were some temporary
denizen nurture and nature can't explain.

between the marsh grass and the dunes,
so I pulled it, though naturally
even out here you tend to wonder
about explosions these days.

Out on the marsh as I tugged
a black-and-white
skull and crossbones stood up—a kite
with red and black streamers.

It climbed a little into the air so I saw
I could fly it if I got it high enough
to catch the breeze. And higher.

I had to get it right this time. Running
across Ferry Street sixty-five years ago
my first kite tore open like tissue before
I even got it to the gate of Glendale Park.

This is the way things will go for you,
a thought told me then, but here
at the other end of my string, the dog
dancing around for me to explain myself,

barking for me to tell him what it was,
the skull and crossbones dancing
up there too—if this is to be my banner, so be it.

NEST

I found it near that corner where
some Septembers a skinny apple tree
hangs fruit the size of stoplights,
the nest itself a palmful,
fallen intact, the bottom so thin
I'd be thinking about
the faith of scarlet tanagers
had I looked up through it
and counted four blue-green eggs
mottled brown, and the nest itself
like a round of serendipity
aspiring to elegance,
tan grasses and a touch of dander
bound with darker rootlets
and *forbs*, meaning any herbs
that aren't grass or grasslike,
another collective name for weeds
like dogshade and rattlebox,
the nest itself hinting toward
the centrifugal, the way things go
when a tree one morning spins
its contents outward.

As though I had walked into some
avian display, it hung on in profile
to the outside of the living-room screen,
hooked in and as still as its effigy,
hoping perhaps to escape notice,
if warblers can hope. Already
betrayed by the white streak of
exclamation below it, a stranger
passing from the Maritimes
to Central America, secretive,
it was not a commonplace pine warbler
who sings like a sewing machine,
or a gaudy yellow-rumped, but perhaps
one of those whose fresh music
can stop me in my tracks. Olive above
and yellow as an Asian pear below,
with an iffy white eye-ring, I found it
in the genus *Oporornis*, between
the MacGillivray's and the Connecticut
warblers, not yet into its first winter,
not yet crepe-faced to earn its name.
As it turned I said mourning warbler,
and looking head-on at me, it turned
again and fled for cover into the oaks,
saving me the recurrent heart-work of
trying to muffle it into a towel, or cut it
out of a fruit tree's netting, or scoop it
from the cold belly of the woodstove.

FRAGMENTS

(Against September 11, 2001)

1.

He breezed past me on a bike so thin
it looked bulletproof, another spandex
superhero, I thought, until he came back
slowly, sagging and loud, both hands
on the grips, talking to nobody
on this road given over to birdsong.
Both towers? He was almost screaming now.
Both? Another vacationer losing
his mind at his leisure, until I saw
the headphone clamped to his helmet.

2.

The smell of apples ambushes me
and it's Corn Hill Road again, September,
not the nowhere of my cluttered rage,
the jags of former things
jamming me up. Can a tree—
all wooden pelvic scoops and spine—sinking

among chokecherry and goldenrod
into the marsh's ferment, a leaf-out
flush with fruit, ever say again,
If you would compose obituaries, think on
the way my time keeps coming round?

Come fall the clearnesses simplify.
Out for sunrise this morning,
I was stopped by a single crash,
then silence in the still woods
before the rushing of deer flight,
one white scut briefly, then another
crash. September air
and the sounds amplify.
Where the river goes
under the road, a doe prinked across
the asphalt, then leapt into the poplars
and looked back over itself, all eyes
and ears so I understood at last how deer
and Guernseys can be in the same family.
And it must be this air's
igniting of memory that recalls how
right about here one fall, trundling
the ancient testudo of its shell
like a Roman war machine,
a resident snapping turtle
crossed toward the mud of a deep sleep.
Come winter, the complications come.
There was that bear corpse
at road's edge last February, a grizzly
by its blond pelt, grimed and rimed,
no steel wreckage near it, as if
it had stumbled out from among
the trees to die. A day of rain
reduced it from ice to fact:
trickles of sand and road oils.

HOME IMPROVEMENT

The new owners seem to be adding
a domed colonial blockhouse
to one side of a Bernard Flores
saltbox, up where that stump's
breaking out of the hillside
as though from prehistory.

There's even a new deck for cocktails,
overbuilt beneath so there'll be
no collapse and subsequent lawsuits.
Just about everything's up there
now, including what looks like
a proscenium arch.

Old Bernard was understated,
a fine hand with a blueprint
and hammer. He would never
have crossed Monticello
with Elixachicken like that,

but damned if his signature work
isn't flying out the door
in flinders, and that mangle
of root and branch, that stump

suggests the head of some
twist-horned beast, a cave wall
aurochs or something older,
its tusks or teeth an early stab
at natural selection.

Whose spirit mask,
which of the deadly sins,
might look like that?

There are days when I know
if I could lay down crossties and rails
all the way out the peninsula, I'd go, passing
Taylorville and the Shag Rocks, then into
memory to that reclaimed henhouse
on the Dogtown road. Maybe in a time
slower than now I might learn your patience,
Asberry, and not panic at my misplaced
password list. Your coop might shine again
with a fresh coat of sun-baked white, crow-shadow
crossed, its door open on flawless October
blue and gold, if it hasn't been supplanted
by a summer home the size of Penn Station.

Without punching in any codes,
I'm over the threshold to see you lift
a piece of the white cedar you chunked
out of a swamp back of the cranberry bogs,
fondling it in thick fingers, testing for balance.
Light but densely grained, it will suffer
harder usage than heftier stock. There are days
when I want the smell of fresh shavings before
they're fodder for the potbelly in the corner,
and the faint chicken ambience
of long ago, muted by paint cans shelved
on the walls, and back-puffs from the stove itself.

What will it be today? You seem in no hurry.
A Canada goose half-finished, a snipe
or a whimbrel ready for the pouncing
of a stiff paintbrush? Telltale, humility,
meadow oxeye—some of your birds

were as locally named as flowers. I can still
name them when I can't recall my Jetpack
number, sleep number, Social Security.

One of those drawknives on the wall
will round that cedar to a shape a jackknife
can incise primary feathers in, and a fluted tail.
You sit in a clutter of your own creation,
untroubled by the disorder you've made. Under
a corner's spiderworks, from a box that says
"Sun Ray Steel Wool," a mallard drake stares.

I'm a grown man now, not the little Skeezix
who passed you wrenches when you lay under
your bug-shaped Ford, home after World War II,
but I don't need to know my blood type, license plate,
VIN number on my car. I need something
to lay my hands on, Asberry. Sanding, priming,
blending. Maybe a rasp to take to the head
before it's fitted, or to roughen the breast
so the paint won't reflect water and sun, and spook
a flock. That's how we'll know this one's for
a gunny bag instead of a dentist's foyer. Tell me
whatever will help me lay hold of the day.

MASCOTS

Late, when the clock's numbers
are a red blur, the screech owl
woke me with its baleful
rapid wailing, the bluest,
blackest side of any music
I've heard. I lay there wishing
again for some charm I knew
so I could roll out of bed
and flip one shoe heel up,
or turn my pants pockets
inside out as if to show that owl
there was nothing of mine
it needed, and send it off
through the dark. Even thinking of it
as a shaggy college mascot
with size twelve feet, the kind
they sell in bookstores with
the school's logo on its chest
and eyes like gold saucers
in its cat face is no help when
it wants me to be its mascot,
wants me to sit on the darkest
shelf in its hollow tree somewhere.

SURE THINGS

On the day after All Souls' I go
to pay my taxes. The crow
is waiting on the town hall lawn,
full of flap, shine, and sass,
immune to grievances, withdrawing
a line of sustenance from the soil.

I have already passed the graveyard,
our plot by the fence where
generations of teenagers will bounce
empties off our stone. Nothing
personal, just thinking to insult
death that way. Taxes and death
for sure, but Ben Franklin omitted
the sooty crow, its smudge
always first in the air
after a hurricane.

Trying for a social life, I chat up
the pretty town treasurer, but stick
her pen in my shirt pocket when I fail,
about as welcome as that smutty
forager on the lawn, who taught me
scavenging, and to take a fistful
of complimentary peppermints
against the time when I
will have no time.

And now you have walked into it
and ruined everything—

this spiderwork
strung across the road in the night

sticks to your face like thinnest
strands of egg.

From that tree the spinner
pushed off across air to this bush,

paying out of herself
to entrap that blue something up the road,

that shape on the verge of arrival
where the yellow line dissolves

in fog. You're that blue thing and now
fall can begin: a butterfly

will turn out to be a leaf
drifting away; your footsteps on this road

prefigure the sound of leaves
walking a tree's decline.

Asters at road's edge
turn up blue rays to spot you

in this minnowy light, this fog
with its odor of old books, sermon

and shipwreck collections bearding
the shelves in abandoned houses.

GETTING A LIFT

1.

Why, when the Gulf of Maine is warming faster
than any other body of water on earth,
do I think of Paris after the November 13 attack,
that young couple I watched on TV
crossing the dusk to each other
in the distance beyond a reporter,
their dark clothes turning them
almost silhouettes, all but her white
sneakers that, when he lifted her
as she hugged him, became antic with joy?

2.

Already the cold-loving cod have gone
way north, beyond the Maritimes,
and the Kemp's ridley turtles are riding
the Gulf Stream from their birth sands
in Mexico all the way to a newly
heating Stellwagen Bank, where a north wind
stiffening into winter can drive them
down this bay along with the belief
they're headed south, until they find
barrier beaches they can't negotiate.

3.

Weeks of exposure and hunger, drifting
like loose buoys, stunned with cold,
then fetching up on the low tides, stranded.
But those lovers? Because he had lifted her,

or because this stranger in raingear is
struggling up the beach toward me with
another lift: the nostrils and off-white belly
and dangling forelegs under her arms?
Carrying her difficult dog to her car? No,
two dogs, one on the other, or rather
two Kemp's ridley turtles
as this volunteer closes on me, smiling.

BLOW-INS

If you think it's Brigadoon out here on the coast
after Labor Day, unreachable, or not worth
waiting out the wind and rain, these displacements
will do nothing for you: the ten cattle egrets

patrolling Boat Meadow Creek like spirits
from the Barbados livestock grazings,
for instance. You wouldn't notice what's blown
north and south. Not down at the tail end of
the outer Hebrides, on Mingulay, but here—

a northern lapwing. Common enough
among the tumbled stones of a nineteenth-
century village, and the vestigial lazy beds
where monks tended crops a thousand years ago,

but here this morning, driven out of the marshes
by storm tides. Black-and-white, too small for
an oystercatcher: lapwing, plover of northern Europe,
unwilling passenger of a November blow.

And who shall say we live in unimportant places
when far from Pontchartrain a brown pelican
crowns a wharf spile as though waiting for
a sculptor of totem poles to work
his way up the bole to it?

When we were young and you dressed
for dinner parties, your entrance
was like the opening of *The Loretta
Young Show.*
            Today I thought of that
and how it dates me, as I went through
your five-foot recipe shelf, looking
for pumpkin pie directions to rescue

the golden pulp I scooped and froze
last fall from the one its vine
had plumped on the bottom step
of the shed so I couldn't miss it.

Those stapled fund-raiser cookbooks
have aged as pathetically
as my old poetry chapbooks.
In time even the names of the cooks
under the concoctions changed,
even the recipes' names. Here's
"Almost as Good as Robert Redford,"
and "Cape Cod Turkey,"
which requires salted fish.

Forget *Rehschlegel* and *Kartoffelsalat,*
but I was the only one who could read your
American handwriting on the loose scraps
and pages stuffing your notebooks,
and translate it for family
to pass on after you'd gone.

Remember checking our secret spot
by the jetty for scallops the storms wash up
around Thanksgiving? Unlocking the oysters
and freeing lobsters from their red armor,

almost fifty years of our Irish-Jewish paella,
and how I'd set bricks under the table legs
to raise it so your back wouldn't ache
during the two weeks you made gift cookies
for our twin feast of lights?

A dozen bubble-wrapped packages of *kavel koko*
and Linzer tortes, rum balls, macaroons, filberts
went to the P.O., and you'd deliver
a plate to the grumpiest neighbor.

Even after your wheelchair, when we'd
read instructions from two different recipes
mistakenly to each other, we found
we could save the results by pouring chocolate
over them, calling them man-cave cookies.
I was glad to take the heat for those. What
a matched set, what a pair, we were.

SENTRY

Thistle, you look like another
of evolution's jokes, impossible
as a great blue heron seems
impossible, though you both
are brilliant survivors.

Still, mixed metaphor,
it looks like someone
hung you all over with
shaving brushes nobody
soft-handed could wield,

then loaded one of those
salad shooters they
used to hawk on TV
and fired green sickles
and scimitars at you,

until, sentry at my door,
you look like a gallowglass
loyal to no one but your own
stickle-backed containment.

I dubbed you Captain Barfoot,
though I know from long
acquaintance that a change
of air will turn you to a mentor

white and silken, proof
that the pilgrim in us all
must cede his spines
and hackers to endure.

Right after Christmas, off the beach,
the windless bay calm as an ice rink,
two black objects low on the waterline,
the larger and longer trailing
the smaller, casually afloat.

Not birds, not arching and wheeling
as dolphins do, and not seals, who may pause
and raise their heads to take a walker in,
even stay parallel to the shore with him
as if greetings might happen.

The weekly *Coastal Reporter* announced
the arrival: the forty-four-year-old mother,
Wart, named for her markings,
with her calf of less than a month, her seventh,
and the earliest right whale birth
on record for this bay.

That morning there had been no breaching
or slapping, only logging, resting calmly adrift,
perhaps so she might coax
her ungainly swimmer to nurse.

What are the chances, with a few hundred
right whales left in the world? At the right place
there is no such time as off-season, and when
the experts rate you functionally
extinct, remember old mamma Wart
and her children, and go with instinct.

ACKNOWLEDGMENTS

Thanks to the editors of the following publications, in which some of the poems in this collection first appeared: *Blackbird, Cold Mountain Review, Epoch, Gettysburg Review, Hudson Review, Hurakan, Ibbetson Street, Kenyon Review, Northeast, The Norton Anthology of American Literature* (seventh edition), *OnEarth, Plume, Poetry, Post Road, Sewanee Review, Shenandoah, Tar River Poetry,* and *32 Poems.*

In "Seeing Stars," the French epigraph from Philippe Claudel translates to "I have discovered that the dead never leave the living."

OTHER BOOKS IN THE CRAB ORCHARD SERIES IN POETRY

Dots & Dashes
Jehanne Dubrow

The Star-Spangled Banner
Denise Duhamel

Smith Blue
Camille T. Dungy

Seam
Tarfia Faizullah

Beautiful Trouble
Amy Fleury

Sympathetic Magic
Amy Fleury

Soluble Fish
Mary Jo Firth Gillett

Pelican Tracks
Elton Glaser

Winter Amnesties
Elton Glaser

Strange Land
Todd Hearon

Always Danger
David Hernandez

Heavenly Bodies
Cynthia Huntington

Terra Nova
Cynthia Huntington

Zion
TJ Jarrett

Red Clay Suite
Honorée Fanonne Jeffers

Fabulae
Joy Katz

Cinema Muto
Jesse Lee Kercheval

Train to Agra
Vandana Khanna

The Primitive Observatory
Gregory Kimbrell

If No Moon
Moira Linehan

Incarnate Grace
Moira Linehan

For Dust Thou Art
Timothy Liu

Strange Valentine
A. Loudermilk

Dark Alphabet
Jennifer Maier